"Oh Dear! Oh Dear! I shall be too late!"

Alice in Wonderland, 1910

MABEL LUCIE ATTWELL

Women Illustrators
of the Golden Age

Edited by
Mary Carolyn Waldrep

Dover Publications
Garden City, New York

OPPOSITE:

After waiting till she fancied she heard the Rabbit just under the window,
she suddenly spread out her hand, and made a snatch in the air.
She heard a little shriek and a fall, and a crash of broken glass.

Alice in Wonderland, 1916

MARGARET WINIFRED TARRANT

Bibliographical Note

This Dover edition, first published in 2010, is an original compilation
of illustrations from various sources.

Library of Congress Cataloging-in-Publication Data

Women illustrators of the golden age / edited by Mary Carolyn Waldrep.—Dover ed.
    p. cm.
    An original compilation of illustrations from various sources.
    Includes bibliographical references.
    ISBN-13: 978-0-486-47252-2
    ISBN-10: 0-486-47252-3
    1. Illustration of books—19th century. 2. Illustration of books—20th century. 3. Magazine
illustration—19th century. 4. Magazine illustration—20th century. 5. Women illustrators.
I. Waldrep, Mary Carolyn.

NC960.B9 2010
741.6—dc22

2010003071

Manufactured in the United States of America
47252305   2021
www.doverpublications.com

Publisher's Note

In the late nineteenth and early twentieth centuries, there was an explosion of newspapers, periodicals, and books. Several factors provided the impetus for this: The rise of the middle class assured a literate and affluent audience; improved transportation systems made widespread distribution possible; and the nineteenth century saw enormous technological advances in printing.

This printed material informed and entertained, just as films, radio, television, and the Internet would do in later decades. A large part of the appeal of this—the first mass media—were the illustrations it offered. Like later media, it influenced, as well as reflected, the society it served. In the 1880s, Kate Greenaway's drawings of charmingly clad children caused a minor revolution in children's fashions; Charles Dana Gibson's "Gibson Girl" created the ideal for young women of the Gilded Age; the paintings of Jessie Willcox Smith served as the standard for American children of the teens and twenties; and the nurseries of Great Britain were filled with the tea sets, dolls, calendars, and prints of Mabel Lucie Attwell.

At the beginning of the nineteenth century, the primary method of reproducing pictures was wood engraving, developed by Thomas Bewick in the latter half of the eighteenth century. In this process, the image was drawn directly on the wood block, then carefully cut away by the engraver. The process was slow; the size of the art limited, and reproduction was in one color only. In the 1850s, Englishman Edmund Evans developed a method of wood engraving that allowed for multi-color printing, and many of Evans' artists—Walter Crane, Randolph Caldecott, and Kate Greenaway—enjoyed enormous success. The invention of photography further advanced the printing process. By the beginning of the twentieth century, lithography had replaced wood engraving as a method of reproducing illustrations.

Printing technology in the United States lagged far behind that in England. Although newspapers and periodicals featured pictures of battle scenes during the American Civil War, the quality of the illustrations was poor. Nevertheless, the public's appetite for artwork had been whetted. In addition, the introduction of public education led to increased literacy, with a subsequent demand for reading material. Where in 1865, some seven hundred periodicals were being published in the United States, by the beginning of the twentieth century, there were over 5,000. The establishment of libraries further increased the market. By the end of the nineteenth century, America had 33 million volumes in 4,000 libraries—more than 2½ times the number of volumes a mere twenty years earlier. Despite this great demand, wood engraving remained the predominant printing method in the United States until the 1880s. Once change came however, it came swiftly. By the end of World War I, America had firmly established itself as a leader in the field of publishing.

During this Victorian era, there was a growing

popularity of books for children. Although the first books geared to children were published centuries earlier, these had been limited to cautionary tales and moral lessons. The children's book as entertainment was born in the 1750s, when John Newbery's Juvenile Library offered abridged versions of classic tales. As the idea that childhood was a separate state from adulthood and should be "fun" became entrenched in the Victorian era, the demand for toys and books for children grew rapidly.

An interest in stories of exotic places, heroic legends of earlier times, and folk and fairy tales became widespread during the Victorian period, both for children and adults, perhaps as a reaction to the drabness of the Industrial Age.

This great proliferation of illustrated material led to an increased demand for illustrators to supply the art. A surprising number of these illustrators were women—in America alone, some eighty women illustrators are known to have been active during this time.

In many ways, illustration seemed a perfect choice as a career for a woman—a knowledge of drawing, along with music and needlework, was a desirable "feminine" accomplishment, and part of the standard education of the middle- and upper-class woman; moreover, illustration could be practiced at home, without interfering with a woman's "real" role as wife and mother. However, this rosy view is far from accurate.

The minimal knowledge of art gained as a part of a young lady's education was not enough to support a career, and educational opportunities in art, as in other fields, were limited for women in the Victorian era. In the mid- to late-nineteenth century, however, several art and design schools specifically for women opened their doors, and still other schools began to admit women. In Great Britain, for example, there was London's Female School of Design, the Lambeth School of Art and Design, and the Slade School of Art, among others. In the United States, you had the Pennsylvania Academy of the Fine Arts and the Drexel Institute of Arts and Sciences in Philadelphia, New York's Cooper Union Free Art School and Brooklyn's Pratt Institute. And no discussion of illustration in America is complete

without mention of Howard Pyle, for no figure is more important to its development, and particularly to the training of female artists. A prolific and talented artist himself, Pyle was also a gifted teacher. Originally on the faculty of Drexel, he opened his own school in

The Little Green Road to Fairyland, 1922
IDA RENTOUL OUTHWAITE

Wilmington, Delaware, in 1900. Nearly half of the students in his first class were women, and during the course of his teaching career, he trained sixty female illustrators, including Jessie Willcox Smith, Elizabeth Shippen Green, and Violet Oakley.

Moreover, the view that a career in illustration was compatible with being a wife and mother was simply not borne out by the facts. In reality, many a talented illustrator, even one who had gained a measure of professional recognition, either gave up her career entirely or drastically curtailed it after marriage. In 1904, Howard Pyle, himself, frustrated after observing this phenomenon, refused to accept any more women students, stating:

The pursuit of art interferes with a girl's social life and destroys her chances of getting married. Girls are, after all, at best, only qualified for sentimental work.[1]

Even Jessie Willcox Smith was quoted as saying:

> . . . if [a woman] elects to be a housewife and mother—that is her sphere, and no other. Circumstances may, but volition should not, lead her from it.
>
> If on the other hand she elects to go into business or the arts, she must sacrifice motherhood in order to fill successfully her chosen sphere.[2]

In fact, it was a rare woman indeed who successfully combined family and career, although women who married artists seem to have fared the best, gaining a partner who understood the pressures of deadlines.

What qualities, then, *did* explain the success of women in the field of illustration? Interestingly, the perception that illustration was an inferior cousin of fine art, worked in their favor—since illustration wasn't "real" art, it was suitable for "mere" women. According to Frances W. Marshall, assistant editor of *St. Nicholas Magazine*,

> As illustrators, women find themselves in a profession where they stand shoulder to shoulder with their brothers in art. For the publisher, the advertiser, the seller of prints and picture cards is interested only in the finished product, and has no concern whatever as to the sex of the producer.[3]

She goes on to state:

> In this career the natural adaptability of woman is a decided advantage. For an illustrator must be biddable, willing to follow the author's lead, and subordinate the expression of her own personality to the text which her pictures accompany. . . .

The Now-a-Days Fairy Book, 1911
JESSIE WILLCOX SMITH

> . . . [this] does not mean that women must extinguish originality, . . . On the contrary, originality is the trait that most often shortens the road to success. . . Their work demands a certain power of impersonation, the ability to lose one's self in a character and experience, the emotion the person in the story or the poem is supposed to feel at the moment in which he is represented in the picture.

The rewards for those who stayed the course were substantial. In America, the average illustrator made $4,000 per year, and could earn anywhere from $10,000 up to $75,000. Not surprisingly, women illustrators were most often assigned themes relating to home and children, sentimental tales, romances, and fairy tales. It is unclear whether this was purely a case of stereotyping, or whether many of the women preferred such subjects. Certainly Willcox Smith showed a definite predilection for pictures of children.

Some of the women featured in this book—Jessie Willcox Smith, Elizabeth Shippen Green, Mabel Lucie

1 Howard Pyle, "Why Art and Marriage Won't Mix," *The North American,* June 19, 1904.
2 Holograph manuscript, noted to possibly be from Louise Armstrong, n.d., Pennsylvania Academy of Art Archives.
3 "Qualities that Make for Success in Women Illustrators," *New York Times,* December 15, 1912.

Attwell, Ida Rentoul Outhwaite, for example—were well-known personalities of their time and had long and illustrious careers. For others, although their name is attached as illustrator of many books spanning a number of years, finding biographical information is extremely difficult. For example, Blanche Fisher Wright, illustrator of *The Real Mother Goose*, which has never been out of print since its publication in 1916, proved particularly elusive. In part, this difficulty is due to the circumstances mentioned before—the tendency of a female illustrator to cease or interrupt her career upon marriage, thus making her more difficult to trace under her maiden name.

During Great Britain's "Golden Age of Illustration," the deluxe gift book, ostensibly for children, lavishly illustrated and elegantly bound, showcased the talents of a number of illustrators. The American Golden Age of Illustration, encompassing the years from the 1880s through the 1930s, includes magazine and advertising illustration as well as book illustration. The 22 artists featured here are but a sampling of the many talented women who participated.

Bibliography

Carter, Alice A., *The Red Rose Girls: an Uncommon Story of Art and Love*, H.N. Abrams, New York, 2000.

Copans, Ruth, "Dream Blocks: American Women Illustrators of the Golden Age, 1890–1920," *Book Illustrated: Text, Image, and Culture, 1770–1930*, Oak Knoll Press, New Castle, Delaware, 2000.

Dalby, Richard, *The Golden Age of Children's Book Illustration*, Michael O'Mara Books Limited, London, 1991.

Goodman, Helen, "Women Illustrators of the Golden Age of American Illustration, *Woman's Art Journal, Vol. I, No. 1* (Spring–Summer, 1987).

Hearn, Michael Patrick, Clark, Trinkett and Clark, H. Nichols B., *Myth, Magic, and Mystery: One Hundred Years of American Children's Book Illustration*, Roberts Rinehart Publishers, Boulder, Colorado, 1996.

Jacobs, Mary Rosalind, *Florence Harrison*, www.florenceharrison.com

Kooistra, Lorraine Janzen, *Christina Rossetti and Illustration: a Publishing History*, Ohio University Press, Athens, Ohio, 2002.

Meyer, Susan E., *A Treasury of the Great Children's Book Illustrators*, Abradale Press, Harry N. Abrams, Inc., Publishers, New York, 1987.

Muir, Marcie and Holden, Robert, *The Fairy World of Ida Rentoul Outhwaite*, Craftsman House, Sydney, 1985.

Ortakales, Denise, *Women Children's Book Illustrators*, www.ortakales.com

Peppin, Brigid and Micklethwait, Lucy, *Book Illustrators of the Twentieth Century*, Arco Publishing, Inc., New York, 1984.

Artists & Volumes

Marigold Garden, 1885

Kate Greenaway
1846–1901

One of the first women to earn a living as an illustrator, Kate Greenaway was born in London. Her father was a wood engraver, and she studied art at the National Art Training School, Heatherley's School of Fine Art, and the Slade School. She did a great deal of magazine work in the 1870s, several books for the publishers, Griffith and Farran, as well as books, greeting cards, and calendars for Marcus Ward.

In 1877, her father showed her sketches and verses to Edmund Evans, who, in association with George Routledge, published them as *Under the Window* in time for Christmas, 1878. The book was an immediate success. Taking the past as her inspiration, Greenaway created a idealized vision of childhood that captured the imagination of the public. By the mid-1880s, she was at the height of her success and Greenaway dolls, wallpaper, fabrics, christening sets, fashions, and other items were manufactured at home in England and abroad.

Under the Window, 1879

Kate Greenaway's Birthday Book, 1880

Kate Greenaway's Birthday Book, 1880

Pied Piper of Hamelin, 1888

KATE GREENAWAY

Little Ann and Other Poems, 1883

Mother Goose or the Old Nursery Rhymes, 1881

Language of Flowers, 1884

Language of Flowers, 1884

KATE GREENAWAY

Marigold Garden, 1885

Under the Window, 1879

Marigold Garden, 1885

Kate Greenaway

"The World," *Shorter Poems by Christina Rossetti*, 1923

Florence Harrison
Active 1887–1937

Florence Harrison is best known for her work for the Scottish publishing firm of Blackie and Sons for whom she illustrated some fifty books. When she began her association with the firm, she incorporated elements of the Glasgow decorative style into her own Pre-Raphaelite work.

Harrison was the first woman to illustrate a commercial edition of Christina Rossetti's work. Living in Chelsea in London when she received the commission, she was commissioned to produce twenty-four full-page color plates, forty-eight full-page black-and-white plates, 120 headpieces and incidental pieces, and a cover. After two years of work, she produced thirty-six color plates and thirty-six black-and-white plates.

Little is known about her personal life, although she is known to have exhibited at the Royal Gallery in London from 1887–1891. Until recently, she was believed to be Emma Florence Harrison, who studied painting at the Glasgow School of Art, but recent evidence discovered by Mary Rosalind Jacobs of England suggests that she was an Australian artist named Florence Susan Harrison.

Strike the bells wantonly

"A Peal of Bells," *Shorter Poems by Christina Rossetti*, 1923

FLORENCE HARRISON

In the room centre stood her husband

"The Ghost's Petition," *Shorter Poems by Christina Rossetti*, 1923

FLORENCE HARRISON

And summer friend has fled

"Songs in a Cornfield," *Shorter Poems by Christina Rossetti,* 1923

FLORENCE HARRISON

White and golden Lizzie stood

"Goblin Market," *Goblin Market and Other Poems by Christina Rossetti*, n.d.

FLORENCE HARRISON

Pale spirits, wailing

"Sleep at Sea," *Goblin Market and Other Poems by Christina Rossetti*, n.d.

FLORENCE HARRISON

She stood on inner ground that budded flowers

"From House to Home," *Goblin Market and Other Poems by Christina Rossetti*, n.d.

FLORENCE HARRISON

My heart is like a singing bird

"A Birthday," *Goblin Market and Other Poems by Christina Rossetti*, n.d.

FLORENCE HARRISON

The Tale of Peter Rabbit, 1902

Beatrix Potter

1866–1943

Beatrix Potter, an only child, was born in Kensington in London. From an early age, she loved painting and drawing, particularly animals and plants.

The Tale of Peter Rabbit, complete with pen-and-ink drawings, first appeared in a letter to a friend. In 1901, unable to find a publisher for the work, she redrew Peter Rabbit and printed 250 black-and-white copies privately. A second edition, with a slightly amended text, appeared a few months later. The publishing firm of Frederick Warne became interested in the book, and released a color edition in 1902. Over 50,000 copies were sold within a year. By 1913, she had produced eighteen books.

The Tale of Squirrel Nutkin, 1903

The Tale of Benjamin Bunny, 1904

The Tale of Tom Kitten, 1907

The Tale of Jemima Puddle-Duck, 1908

BEATRIX POTTER

14

The Tale of the Flopsy Bunnies, 1909

BEATRIX POTTER

The Tale of Timmy Tiptoes, 1911

The Tale of Mr. Tod, 1912

The Tale of Mr. Tod, 1912

The Tale of Pigling Bland, 1913

BEATRIX POTTER

"The Little Mermaid"
The Fairy Tales of Hans Christian Andersen, 1899

Helen Stratton

Active 1892–1924

British illustrator Helen Stratton worked primarily with fairy tales and legends. Her bold Art Nouveau style is often compared to that of Arthur Hughes, W. Heath Robinson, and J. D. Batten. She produced at least five editions of Hans Christian Andersen's tales for Blackie and Son between 1896 and 1908, the most notable being the 1899 edition, featuring more than 400 pen-and-ink illustrations.

Other books illustrated by Stratton include 1899's *The Arabian Nights Entertainments* (on which she collaborated with Robinson and other artists), *Grimm's Fairy Tales* (1903), George MacDonald's *The Princess and the Goblin* (1911) and *The Princess and Curdie* (1912).

It was the old soldier

"The Red Shoes," *The Fairy Tales of Hans Christian Andersen,* 1899

HELEN STRATTON

There were evolutions for you!

"The Storks," *The Fairy Tales of Hans Christian Andersen*, 1899

HELEN STRATTON

There came a knock at the town gate, and the old king went and opened it

"The Real Princess," *The Fairy Tales of Hans Christian Andersen*, 1899

HELEN STRATTON

The desire to fight with him was gone

Heroic Legends, n.d.

HELEN STRATTON

Sir La-Cote-Male-Taile chooses a bride

Heroic Legends, n.d.

HELEN STRATTON

"Tiphaiine la Fée," *Harper's Monthly Magazine*, April 1906

Elizabeth Shippen Green
1871–1954

One of the most successful illustrators of her time, American artist Elizabeth Shippen Green studied at the Pennsylvania Academy of Fine Arts under Thomas Eakins, Thomas Anshutz, and Robert Vonnoh. She sold her first illustration at age eighteen to the *Philadelphia Times*, and was working at the *Saturday Evening Post* and *Ladies' Home Journal* when she began her studies with Howard Pyle at the Drexel Institute. While at Drexel, she met fellow artists Jessie Willcox Smith and Violet Oakley, with whom she would share a home for fourteen years.

In 1901, Green became the first woman staff artist for *Harper's* magazine, an association that lasted until 1924. She married artist and educator Huger Elliott in 1911, and moved with him several times as his career dictated. Despite these moves, Green's career never faltered. In fact, she actually produced more art *after* her marriage than before. Her career spanned over forty years and her work appeared in over thirty books and countless magazines.

Jehane—The Constant Lover

"The Navarrese," *Harper's Monthly Magazine*, September 1906

ELIZABETH SHIPPEN GREEN

Miguela, Kneeling Still, Put it to her Lips

"The Spanish Jade," *Harper's Monthly Magazine,* September 1906

ELIZABETH SHIPPEN GREEN

Gisele

Harper's Monthly Magazine, October 1908

ELIZABETH SHIPPEN GREEN

The child was sitting in a patch of sunshine

The Flowers, 1910

ELIZABETH SHIPPEN GREEN

The Journey

The Book of the Little Past, 1912

ELIZABETH SHIPPEN GREEN

The Everyday Fairy Book, 1915

Jessie Willcox Smith
1863–1935

American artist Jessie Willcox Smith was destined for a career as a kindergarten teacher when she discovered her artistic talent while chaperoning a friend at an art lesson. In 1884, she entered the School of Design for Women in Philadelphia, concentrating her studies on commercial art. She transferred to the Pennsylvania Academy of Fine Arts in 1885, where she studied with Thomas Eakins and Thomas Anschutz. She published her first drawing in *St. Nicholas* magazine in 1888. She then joined the advertising department of *Ladies' Home Journal*, where she worked until 1898. In 1894, she joined Howard Pyle's first class at Drexel Institute of Arts and Sciences, where she first met Elizabeth Shippen Green and Violet Oakley, with whom she became lifelong friends.

During her career, she illustrated nearly forty books, including Robert Louis Stevenson's *A Child's Garden of Verses* (1905), and Charles Kingsley's *The Water Babies* (1916), a book that is considered by many to be her masterpiece. She also created numerous advertisements, worked for all of the major periodicals of the day, and accepted private portrait commissions. From 1918 to 1933, her paintings appeared on every cover of *Good Housekeeping Magazine*, earning her a quarter of a million dollars.

"Are you ill, dear North Wind?"

At the Back of the North Wind, 1919

JESSIE WILLCOX SMITH

"Oh, don't hurt me!"

The Water Babies, 1916

JESSIE WILLCOX SMITH

Mrs. Doasyouwouldbedoneby

The Water Babies, 1916

Jessie Willcox Smith

Beauty and the Beast

The Now-a-Days Fairy Book, 1911

JESSIE WILLCOX SMITH

Robin put his head down on his arm and shut his eyes

The Now-a-Days Fairy Book, 1911

Jessie Willcox Smith

Alice in Wonderland

Boys and Girls of Bookland, 1923

JESSIE WILLCOX SMITH

The Flowers

A Child's Garden of Verses, 1905

JESSIE WILLCOX SMITH

"The Young King," *A House of Pomegranates*, n.d.

Jessie Marion King
1875–1949

Jessie Marion King entered the Glasgow School of Art in 1891, where she came in contact with the work of Charles Rennie Macintosh and other Arts and Crafts artists. She traveled to France and Italy on a scholarship from the school, and, while in Italy, first encountered the paintings of Botticelli, which were to have a strong influence on her work. Although definitely in the Glasgow style, her delicate pen-and-ink drawings, often with color washes, were highly individual.

In addition to being a talented illustrator, King was an accomplished designer of books, jewelry, textiles, and costume. In 1899 she received a commission from a Berlin department store to design items in the new "Scottish style." In 1902, she received a gold medal for her book design of *L'Evangile de l'Enfance* in the International Exhibition of Decorative Arts in Turin. That same year she began teaching book design at the Glasgow School.

She married fellow artist E. A. Taylor in 1908, and moved with him to Paris in 1910, where they ran a studio gallery. They returned to Scotland at the outbreak of World War I and settled in the artist community of Kirkcudbright, where King started a center for women artists.

In her hand she had a spray of wild hemlock that was blossoming

"The Fisherman and His Soul," *A House of Pomegranates,* n.d.

JESSIE MARION KING

I HAD·NEVER·SEEN·ANYONE·SO·PALE

I had never seen anyone so pale

"The Fisherman and His Soul," *A House of Pomegranates,* n.d.

JESSIE MARION KING

Her face was veiled with a veil of gauze but her feet were naked

"The Fisherman and His Soul," *A House of Pomegranates*, n.d.

JESSIE MARION KING

· BVT · ONLY · A · LITTLE · CHILD · WHO · WAS · ASLEEP ·

But only a little child who was asleep

"The Star-Child," *A House of Pomegranates,* n.d.

JESSIE MARION KING

THE · LITTLE · PRINCESS · HAD · ALWAYS · TO · PLAY · ALONE · · ·

The little princess had always to play alone

"The Birthday of the Infanta," *A House of Pomegranates*, n.d.

Jessie Marion King

"The Six Swans," *The Wild Swans and Other Stories,* 1922

Elenore Plaisted Abbott

1875–1935

Elenore Plaisted was born in Maine and studied at the Philadelphia School of Design for Women, the Pennsylvania Academy of Fine Arts, and in Paris. She was already an established illustrator when she entered Howard Pyle's class at Drexel Institute in 1899. Her work appeared in *Leslie's Monthly Magazine, Scribner's, Saturday Evening Post, Harper's,* and other magazines. She illustrated numerous books including Robert Louis Stevenson's *Treasure Island* (1911) and *Kidnapped* (1915), Louisa May Alcott's *An Old-Fashioned Girl,* two volumes of fairy tales by Hans Christian Andersen, and her best-known work, *Grimm's Fairy Tales* (1920).

She was a member of and exhibited with the Plastic Club of Philadelphia and the Philadelphia Water Color Club. She was married to fellow artist C. Yarnall Abbott. In addition to illustration she also did scenic design for what is now the Hedgerow Theatre in Wallingford, Pennsylvania.

"Earth men, come up!"

"The Two Kings' Children," *Grimm's Fairy Tales,* 1920

ELENORE PLAISTED ABBOTT

Rustle and shake yourself, dear tree, / And silver and gold throw down to me

"Cinderella," *Grimm's Fairy Tales,* 1920

ELENORE PLAISTED ABBOTT

The twelve princesses

"The Shoes Which Were Danced to Pieces," *Grimm's Fairy Tales*, 1920

ELENORE PLAISTED ABBOTT

The king's daughter had been carried away by a dragon

"The Four Accomplished Brothers," *Grimm's Fairy Tales*, 1920

Elenore Plaisted Abbott

The maiden thought it was all a dream

"The House in the Wood," *Grimm's Fairy Tales,* 1920

ELENORE PLAISTED ABBOTT

The swans settled close by her

"The Wild Swans," *The Wild Swans and Other Stories*, 1922

ELENORE PLAISTED ABBOTT

The fish swam right up to the little mermaid princess

"The Mermaid," *The Flower Maiden and Other Stories*, 1922

ELENORE PLAISTED ABBOTT

Peter Pan and Wendy, 1921

Mabel Lucie Attwell
1879–1964

Born in London, Mabel Lucie Attwell studied at both the Regent School of Art and Heatherley's School of Art. She began her professional career at sixteen when she submitted several drawings to an artist's agency in London. Her early career concentrated on magazine work, but by 1900, she had begun to illustrate books. From 1905 to 1913, she illustrated ten books for W. & R. Chambers. One of her most successful books was *Alice in Wonderland* in 1910 for Raphael Tuck, for whom she also illustrated *Hans Andersen's Fairy Tales* (1914), and Charles Kingsley's *The Water Babies* (1916), among others. J. M. Barrie was an admirer of her work, and personally asked her to illustrate Hodder & Stoughton's gift edition of his *Peter Pan and Wendy* in 1921.

Like many female illustrators, Attwell specialized in drawing children. Her chubby-cheeked toddlers proved extraordinarily popular with the public and she became a household name in the 1920s, '30s, and '40s. In addition to books and magazines, Attwell designed postcards and greeting cards for Valentine & Sons as well as plaques, posters, calendars, tea sets, dolls, figurines, and dozens of other products.

"The Tinder-Box," *Hans Andersen's Fairy Tales*, 1914

MABEL LUCIE ATTWELL

"The Little Mermaid," *Hans Andersen's Fairy Tales,* 1914

MABEL LUCIE ATTWELL

"The Little Match Girl," *Hans Andersen's Fairy Tales*, 1914

MABEL LUCIE ATTWELL

The home in the ground

Peter Pan and Wendy, 1921

MABEL LUCIE ATTWELL

The rabbit started violently

Alice in Wonderland, 1910

MABEL LUCIE ATTWELL

The mock turtle's story

Alice in Wonderland, 1910

MABEL LUCIE ATTWELL

The pig baby

Alice in Wonderland, 1910

MABEL LUCIE ATTWELL

Fairy Islands, *Elves and Fairies,* 1916

Ida Rentoul Outhwaite

1888–1960

Ida Rentoul Outhwaite was born near Melbourne, Australia. She and her elder sister Annie began contributing stories to local magazines in 1903 and published their first book, *Mollie's Bunyip,* in 1904 when Ida was just sixteen years old. Her books were among the first children's books to be set in Australia. She married Grenbry Outhwaite in 1909. Much of her success is due to his efforts in managing her career and he wrote the texts for several of her books.

Elves and Fairies (1916), written by Annie and illustrated by Ida, was one of the first color books published in Australia, and the first major Australian gift book to equal the quality of the British deluxe editions.

In 1920, Outhwaite held an exhibition of her work in London, and began her association with the publisher A. & C. Black. Black published five gift book productions of her fairy paintings between 1921 and 1930: *The Enchanted Forest* (1921), *The Little Green Road to Fairyland* (1922), *The Little Fairy Sister* (1923), all with accompanying texts by her sister and husband, and *Blossom,* and *Bunny and Brownie,* which Ida wrote herself. *The Little Green Road to Fairyland* was one of the best-loved Australian children's books from the 1920s through the 1950s.

Moonboat, *Elves and Fairies*, 1916

IDA RENTOUL OUTHWAITE

Moonrise, *Elves and Fairies*, 1916

Ida Rentoul Outhwaite

The Jazz Band

The Enchanted Forest, 1921

IDA RENTOUL OUTHWAITE

Anne plays the pipes

The Enchanted Forest, 1921

IDA RENTOUL OUTHWAITE

She flew through the window, with Gumkin close behind

The Little Green Road to Fairyland, 1922

IDA RENTOUL OUTHWAITE

Sylvie in her fairy frock floating on the great bubble

The Little Green Road to Fairyland, 1922

IDA RENTOUL OUTHWAITE

"I am Kexy, friend of fairies"

The Little Green Road to Fairyland, 1922

IDA RENTOUL OUTHWAITE

A Child's Garden of Verses, 1919

Ruth Mary Hallock
1876–1945

Ruth Mary Hallock was born in Erie, Pennsylvania, and attended the Art Institute of Chicago. There she studied under Matilda Vanderpool, Frederick W. Freer, and Robert Blum, and was a participant in the school's Ninth Annual Exhibition in March of 1903. By 1904, she had a number of illustrated books to her credit—for example, *Stony Lonesome* by Arthur J. Russell, *The Story of a Short Life* by Juliana H. Ewing, and *Everyday Essays* by Marion Forster Washburne. Much of her work was done for the education market and she contributed illustrations to numerous readers and primers. Although she had an active career through the 1930s, Robert Louis Stevenson's *A Child's Garden of Verses,* published in 1919, is her best-known work.

"Foreign Children," *A Child's Garden of Verses,* 1919

Ruth Mary Hallock

I saw you toss the kites on high / And blow the birds about the sky

"The Wind," *A Child's Garden of Verses,* 1919

RUTH MARY HALLOCK

The rain is raining all around

"The Rain," *A Child's Garden of Verses,* 1919

RUTH MARY HALLOCK

Happy hearts and happy faces, / Happy play in grassy places

"Good and Bad Children," *A Child's Garden of Verses,* 1919

RUTH MARY HALLOCK

The world is so full of a number of things, / I'm sure we should all be as happy as kings

"Happy Thought," *A Child's Garden of Verses,* 1919

RUTH MARY HALLOCK

"Sicilianisch"
Schumann Album of Children's Pieces for Piano, n.d.

Henriette Willebeek Le Mair

1889–1966

Henriette Willebeek Le Mair was born in Rotterdam to a wealthy family. Her parents were artists and often wrote verses for her to illustrate. Her first book, *Première Rondes Enfantines,* was published in France in 1904, when she was fifteen. In her early twenties, she opened an art school in her home and many of her students became models for her watercolor drawings.

Beginning in 1911, she published a number of books with the music publishers Augener, including *Our Old Nursery Rhymes* (1911), *Little Songs of Long Ago* (1912), *The Children's Corner* (1914), *Little People* (1915), and *Old Dutch Nursery Rhymes* (1917). She also illustrated *A Gallery of Children* with a text by A. A. Milne in 1925 and Robert Louis Stevenson's *A Child's Garden of Verses* in 1926.

Le Mair had a great interest in Eastern philosophy, and she and her husband, Baron van Tuyll van Serooskerken, converted to Sufism in the 1920s.

"Humpty Dumpty," *Our Old Nursery Rhymes,* 1911

"Mary, Mary, Quite Contrary," *Our Old Nursery Rhymes,* 1911

Henriette Willebeek Le Mair

"At the Seaside," *A Child's Garden of Verses,* 1926

HENRIETTE WILLEBEEK LE MAIR

"The Land of Nod," *A Child's Garden of Verses,* 1926

HENRIETTE WILLEBEEK LE MAIR

"Armies in the Fire," *A Child's Garden of Verses,* 1926

HENRIETTE WILLEBEEK LE MAIR

"Time to Rise," *A Child's Garden of Verses,* 1926

HENRIETTE WILLEBEEK LE MAIR

"The Swing," *A Child's Garden of Verses*, 1926

Henriette Willebeek Le Mair

"The Land of Counterpane," *A Child's Garden of Verses,* 1926

Henriette Willebeek Le Mair

Alice in Wonderland, 1916

Margaret Winifred Tarrant

1888–1959

Margaret Tarrant was the daughter of landscape painter and illustrator Percy Tarrant. She followed in her father's footsteps and began illustrating Christmas cards at age eighteen. Her first book commission was Charles Kingsley's *The Water Babies* in 1908 when she was twenty, and she was already an established illustrator when she began her art studies at Heatherley's School of Art. She illustrated books for a number of different publishers, and also produced postcards, calendars, greeting cards, and prints. Books illustrated by her include Lewis Carroll's *Alice in Wonderland* (1916), Robert Browning's *The Pied Piper of Hamelin* (1912), and Harry Golding's *Zoo Days* (1919). In 1920, she began an association with the Medici Society, for whom she produced a very popular series of flower fairy books.

Alice in Wonderland, 1916

MARGARET WINIFRED TARRANT

Alice in Wonderland, 1916

MARGARET WINIFRED TARRANT

"A long time to wait!"

Zoo Days, 1919

"The sea-lions gave us a lovely ride"

Zoo Days, 1919

MARGARET WINIFRED TARRANT

"Mr. Chimp was reading the newspaper"

Zoo Days, 1919

Margaret Winifred Tarrant

"Full up. Inside only!"

Zoo Days, 1919

Margaret Winifred Tarrant

"The Frog Prince," *Once Upon a Time*, 1921

Margaret Evans Price

1888–1973

Margaret Evans Price was a painter, illustrator, writer, and muralist. She was born in Chicago, but lived most of her life in the eastern United States and Canada. She became interested in art at a very early age and sold her first illustrated story to the *Boston Journal* in 1900. She attended the Massachusetts Normal Art School and the Boston Academy of Fine Arts, and also studied in France. After she completed her studies, she worked as an illustrator for several magazines in New York City.

She married Irving L. Price in 1909. In 1930 her husband, together with Herman G. Fisher, founded the Fisher-Price Toy Company. Margaret became its first Art Director and designed a line of pull-toys based on characters from her children's books.

Her books include *A Visit to Santa Claus* (1916), *Mother Goose Book of Rhymes* (1917), *Once Upon a Time* (1921), *Enchantment Tales for Children* (1926), and *Goody Naughty Book* (1935).

"Beauty and the Beast," *Once Upon a Time*, 1921

MARGARET EVANS PRICE

"Little Red Riding-Hood," *Once Upon a Time*, 1921

MARGARET EVANS PRICE

"Cinderella or the Little Glass Slipper," *Once Upon a Time*, 1921

MARGARET EVANS PRICE

Neptune, god of the sea, was angry with Ulysses

"Nausicaa and Ulysses," *Enchantment Tales for Children,* 1926

MARGARET EVANS PRICE

Circe took an ivory wand in her hand and touched the men one by one

"Circe and Ulysses," *Enchantment Tales for Children*, 1926

MARGARET EVANS PRICE

"The Shoes Which Were Danced to Pieces"
Grimms' Fairy Tales, 1922

Anne Anderson
1874–1930

Anne Anderson was born in Scotland, but spent much of her childhood in Argentina. During her career, she illustrated over one hundred books as well as designing greeting cards. Both Jessie King and Mabel Lucie Attwell were major influences on her work. She married the painter Alan Wright in 1912 and collaborated on several books with him.

Among the books she illustrated are *Aucassin and Nicolette* (1911), *Old French Nursery Songs* (n.d.), the *Cosy-Comfy Book* (1920), *Grimms' Fairy Tales* (1922), and *The Water Babies* (1924).

"The Frog Prince," *Grimms' Fairy Tales,* 1922

ANNE ANDERSON

"The Miller's Daughter," *Grimms' Fairy Tales,* 1922

ANNE ANDERSON

"The House in the Wood," *Grimms' Fairy Tales*, 1922

ANNE ANDERSON

The old toad gave the princess a ploughwheel

"The Iron Stove," *Grimms' Fairy Tales*, 1922

Anne Anderson

"Oh, you beautiful creature!" said Tom

Such a fish! ten times as big as the biggest trout

Tom had never seen a lobster before,
and he was delighted

The ice-fairies, who drive away
the storms and clouds

The Water Babies, 1924

Anne Anderson

The Animal Story Book, 1928

Clara M. Burd

1873–1933

Clara Burd was born in New York City at the home of her paternal grandparents. She attended the National Academy of Design in New York and, in 1898, went to Paris to continue her studies. When she returned to the United States she studied stained glass design at the Tiffany studios in New York and designed numerous church windows as well as a memorial window for President McKinley.

She is best known for her children's book illustrations, but her work also appeared in the leading magazines of the day, such as *Woman's Home Companion, Woman's World, Modern Priscilla,* and *Literary Digest.* Her books include *Threads of Grey and Gold* (1913), *Stories of Great Adventures* (1919), *Hans Brinker or the Silver Skates* (1925), *Little Women* (1926), *The Animal Story Book* (1928), and *A Child's Garden of Verses* (1930).

In her gingham sunbonnet and checked apron
she had been out in the green field among the lambs

The Animal Story Book, 1928

CLARA M. BURD

I tried to coax the cottontails; out in the orchard lot
With my lunch pail I would sit for hours in just the one same spot

The Animal Story Book, 1928

CLARA M. BURD

They came down to feed the ducks and geese every day

The Animal Story Book, 1928

CLARA M. BURD

"Goosey, Goosey, Gander," *The Real Mother Goose*, 1916

Blanche Fisher Wright

Active 1900s–1920s

Although Blanche Fisher Wright is the illustrator of one of America's best-known children's books, *The Real Mother Goose,* information on her life is difficult to find. She is listed as the illustrator of several books as early as 1904 and had numerous titles to her credit, including a number of Mother Goose tales by the time she illustrated *The Real Mother Goose* in 1916. Together with her husband, Broadway actor Charles Laite, in 1925, Ms. Wright became the foster mother of Gordon Laite, who became a well-known illustrator of children's books in the 1960s and '70s. Ms. Wright had at least one brother, Charles Douglas Fisher, who was the founder of a toy company, and one sister, Lola Fisher, an actress.

"The Old Woman Tossed in a Basket," *The Real Mother Goose*, 1916

BLANCHE FISHER WRIGHT

"Mary, Mary, Quite Contrary," *The Real Mother Goose,* 1916

Blanche Fisher Wright

"Snowflakes," *The Peter Patter Book,* 1918

BLANCHE FISHER WRIGHT

"The Wind," *The Peter Patter Book,* 1918

BLANCHE FISHER WRIGHT

"Confidence," *The Peter Patter Book,* 1918

BLANCHE FISHER WRIGHT

The Three Mulla-Mulgars, 1919

Dorothy Pulis Lathrop

1891–1980

Dorothy Pulis Lathrop was born in Albany, New York. She studied art at the Teachers College of Columbia University in New York City and planned a career as an art teacher. She later studied at The Pennsylvania Academy of Fine Arts and the Art Students League in New York City. Her first book, *Japanese Prints,* was published in 1919, although she received no payment for it, as the publisher went bankrupt. Beginning in 1919, she illustrated a new book almost every year, including Walter de la Mare's *The Three Mulla-Mulgars* (1919), George MacDonald's *The Light Princess* (1926) and the *Princess and Curdie* (1927). Rachel Field's *Hitty, Her First Hundred Years,* which received the 1930 Newbery Award is probably her best-known book. In 1938, Lathrop was awarded the first Caldecott Medal for *Animals of the Bible*. In 1931, she began writing as well as illustrating children's books, beginning with *The Fairy Circus*.

He jumped, he reared, he kicked, he plunged, he wriggled, he whinnied

The Three Mulla-Mulgars, 1919

Dorothy Pulis Lathrop

He felt a sudden darkness above his head, and a cold terror crept over his skin

The Three Mulla-Mulgars, 1919

Dorothy Pulis Lathrop

With sticks and staves and flaring torches they turned on the fierce birds
that came sweeping and swirling out of the dark

The Three Mulla-Mulgars, 1919

DOROTHY PULIS LATHROP

The Wonderstone

The Three Mulla-Mulgars, 1919

Dorothy Pulis Lathrop

The Queen of the Mountains is in the forest . . . with fingers of frost

The Three Mulla-Mulgars, 1919

DOROTHY PULIS LATHROP

"Mary Had a Little Lamb," *Mother Goose Rhymes,* 1922

Lois Lenski

1893–1974

Lois Lenski was born in Springfield, Illinois. Her mother was a teacher and her father a Lutheran minister. She received a Bachelor of Science in Education at Ohio State University, but decided to become an artist rather than a teacher. She moved to New York after she received a scholarship to the Art Students League, where she studied illustration with Arthur Covey, whom she would later marry. While still at the Art Students League, she illustrated her first book, a coloring book for Platt & Munk, for which she was paid $100. In 1920, Lenski traveled to London, where she studied at the Westminster School of Art and illustrated three books for the publisher John Lane. At the suggestion of publisher Helen Dean Fish, Lenski began writing her own books. The first, *Skipping Village,* was published in 1927. Her career spanned over fifty years, during which time she wrote and illustrated nearly one hundred of her own books, and illustrated fifty books for other authors.

"Little Bo Peep," *Mother Goose Rhymes*, 1922

Lois Lenski

"Old Mother Hubbard," *Mother Goose Rhymes*, 1922

Lois Lenski

So I was fain to fetch Arthur

The Golden Age, 1921

Lois Lenski

With eyes and fingers we struggled at the decipherment

The Golden Age, 1921

Lois Lenski

For ever ringing an imaginary bell and offering airy muffins
to a bustling, thronging crowd of your own creation

The Golden Age, 1921

Lois Lenski

Old French Fairy Tales, 1920

Virginia Frances Sterrett

1900–1931

Virginia Frances Sterrett was born in Chicago, but spent her early years in Missouri and Kansas. Her father died when she was very young, and the family had little in the way of financial resources.

In 1915, the family moved back to Chicago. She received a scholarship to the Art Institute of Chicago, but had to leave after only fourteen months in order to support her family due to her mother's ill health. Over the next three years, Virginia worked for various advertising agencies in Chicago. Her health, too, began to fail, and she was diagnosed with tuberculosis.

In 1919, she was commissioned by the Penn Publishing Company to provide illustrations for *Old French Fairy Tales* by Comtesse de Segur. Two years later, she illustrated *Tanglewood Tales,* also for Penn.

Sterrett and her family moved to California in 1923, where she entered a sanitorium. She continued to work, but had to limit her working hours due to her health. Penn Publishing hired her for a third book, *Arabian Nights,* which was published in 1928. Soon afterward, her health improved and she left the sanitorium. She had several exhibitions of her work over the next few years, and Penn approached her to illustrate *Myths and Legends.* Although she had finished most of the art for the book, she died before it was completed.

Rosalie saw before her eyes a tree of marvelous beauty

"The Little Gray Mouse," *Old French Fairy Tales,* 1920

VIRGINIA FRANCES STERRETT

They were three months passing through the forest

"Blondine, Bonne-Biche, and Beau-Minon," *Old French Fairy Tales*, 1920

VIRGINIA FRANCES STERRETT

They walked side by side during the rest of the evening

Old French Fairy Tales, 1920

VIRGINIA FRANCES STERRETT

The fairy must give herself up to the queen and lose her power for eight days

"The Princess Rosette"

Violette takes refuge from the wild boar

"Ourson"

Old French Fairy Tales, 1920

VIRGINIA FRANCES STERRETT

Violette consented willingly to pass the night in the forest

"Ourson," *Old French Fairy Tales,* 1920

VIRGINIA FRANCES STERRETT

"Little Miss Muffet," *Mother Goose Rhymes,* 1932

Eulalie Bachmann

1895–1999

Eulalie Bachmann, who published under her first name only, was born in London. Her first picture book, *Bobby in Bubbleland* (1913), was published when she was just eighteen. In 1916, she married Arthur Wilson, a captain in the RAF Expeditionary Force, and in 1918, the couple moved first to Canada, then to the United States. She collaborated with Watty Piper on several fairy-tale books for New York publishers Platt & Munk.

She was divorced in 1931 and moved to California, where she painted murals for Hollywood stars, including Harold Lloyd and Charlie Chaplin. In 1937 she returned to England, where she lived until 1953; she then moved back to California to live until her death. She continued to draw and paint until she was in her nineties and illustrated an impressive number of calendars, magazines, and greeting cards as well as over fifty children's books during her long career.

"Old King Cole," *Mother Goose Rhymes*, 1922

EULALIE BACHMANN

"At the Seaside," *A Child's Garden of Verses*, 1929

Eulalie Bachmann

"Bed in Summer," *A Child's Garden of Verses*, 1929

EULALIE BACHMANN

"Marching Song," *A Child's Garden of Verses,* 1940

Fern Bisel Peat

1893–1971

Fern Bisel Peat was born in Erie, Pennsylvania. She attended Ohio Wesleyan University. She ran an interior decorating studio with her husband, Frank Edwin Peat, specializing in designing children's rooms, murals, children's hospitals, and orphanages as well as textiles and wallpapers. She illustrated several children's books for Samuel Lowe and The Saalfield Publishing Company, for whom she also created paper dolls. She and her husband collaborated on several books of songs for Saalfield. She served as art director for *Children's Playmate* magazine in the 1940s, and created most of its covers.

"Rain," *A Child's Garden of Verses*, 1940

FERN BISEL PEAT

"The Dumb Soldier," *A Child's Garden of Verses*, 1940

FERN BISEL PEAT

"The Night Before Christmas," c. 1936

FERN BISEL PEAT